Montana's
ROCKY
MOUNTAIN
FRONT

TEXT AND PHOTOS BY RICK AND SUSIE GRAETZ

ESSAYS BY GENE SENTZ

The Montana Series

NUMBER FIVE

PHOTOGRAPHY CONTRIBUTIONS BY:

Erwin and Peggy Bauer ▪ Randy Beacham ▪ Douglass Dye
Chuck Haney ▪ John Lambing ▪ Mike Manuel/Fairfield Sun Times ▪ Larry Mayer
Jim Mepham ▪ John Reddy ▪ Ralph Waldt ▪ George Wuerthner

Crown Mountain
from above
Benchmark Road.
RICK AND SUSIE GRAETZ

An old Metis
homestead sits
below the easily
recognized,
Ear Mountain.
RICK AND SUSIE GRAETZ

©2000 Northern Rockies Publishing
Rick and Susie Graetz
P.O. Box 1707, Helena, Montana 59624
norockpub@aol.com

Design by GingerBee Graphics

All color, design and prepress
work done in Montana, U.S.A.
Printed in Korea
Softcover: ISBN 1-89-1152-08-4
Hardcover: ISBN 1-89-1152-11-4

Front Cover:
Lupine flowers and Ear Mountain.
RICK AND SUSIE GRAETZ

THE ROCKY MOUNTAIN FRONT

By Rick and Susie Graetz

Beyond the reach of recorded history, people migrating south from what is now Alaska into what became Montana established a passageway along the eastern flank of an imposing natural barrier. The route is now known as The Old North Trail. Much later, some of the first white travelers heading westward across the wave of the prairie through Montana territory gazed at glistening peaks ahead of them, a commanding sight they called the shining mountains. Today, we refer to this 120-mile stretch of one of the most spectacular pieces of geography on the continent as the Rocky Mountain Front.

Simply put, this is where the plains end and the mountains begin. No transition zone of slowly rising foothills, the mountain wall wastes no space in making its presence felt. And what a presence and treasure. It is fitting that such a magnificent structure serve as the eastern sentinel of the revered Bob Marshall Wilderness.

The spectacular limestone fault scarps and mountains of the Front, rising 2,000 to 4,000 feet, are the gates to the wildlands beyond. Only a few roads intrude a short way into the deep canyons providing access to the wilderness trails. The sights of precipitous reefs, clear streams and lofty peaks of the Rocky Mountain Front offer a proper prelude to the backcountry journey ahead.

This is one side of the land. There is also the softer landscape that flows east. Rippling rounded hills are interspersed with buttes, river bottoms, flatland, clusters of deciduous and conifer trees and wetlands. When coupled with the powerful massif that halts its sweep on the west, the blend is what has inspired people to love and cherish this place.

The brush along the North Fork of Willow Creek is a favorite haunt for grizzlies.
RICK AND SUSIE GRAETZ

The Front is also alive and rich with wildlife, making a home for many species that have disappeared elsewhere. The largest population of grizzly bear and wolverine south of Canada roam here, along with sizable numbers of bighorn sheep. This land is the only place in the lower 48 states where the big bears still venture out to the prairie where they roamed when Lewis and Clark explored Montana. Rocky Mountain gray wolves frequent the northern canyons of the Front range. Small numbers of west slope cutthroat trout, for the most part found only west of the Continental Divide, inhabit some of the streams of the region. The reefs and walls provide sanctuary for bald and golden eagles, prairie falcons and peregrine. The southern reaches serve as prime wintering ground for the huge Sun River elk herd as well as deer and antelope.

Most insignificant of the inhabitants of the Front in relation to the space they occupy is the human species. Hard up against the rise of the mountains, widely separated ranches and a scattering of isolated houses dot the open expanse. A few structures have worked their way into the canyon openings. Otherwise, the immediate Rocky Mountain Front is free of extensive people presence. Even the towns set well to the east of the contact of mountains and plains are unobtrusive. They are pleasant, small communities: Augusta, Choteau, Bynum, Pendroy, Dupuyer, Heart Butte, St. Mary, Browning, Babb and East Glacier, spaced over 152 miles of highway.

Some human activity poses the greatest threat to this special place. The same attributes that cause public outcry to protect it, also attract those who see the splendor of the Rocky Mountain Front only in terms of profit or as a geologic formation to be tapped for its possible extractive benefits. There are those who would subdivide it, explore it for oil and gas, and road it—all for short-term benefit for a few at the expense of the long tenure and integrity of what has often been referred to as "America's Serengetti."

The Rocky Mountain Front has its friends, and they are many, including concerned individuals in the U. S. Forest Service, the Bureau of Land Management, the Blackfeet Tribe, The Nature Conservancy, citizens throughout the nation, and landowners along these mountains. And thanks to these many supporters, the chances that the Front will remain forever unaltered are great. However, it will require constant efforts and vigilance.

Mountain goats.

JIM MEPHAM

This urgent work needs people who understand the infinite value of this majestic piece of our state. Get intimate with it in all seasons and probe its roads and trails. In the long light of a summer evening, watch as all the details of the heights slowly fade, leaving a purple silhouette on the horizon. Catch the first golden light of a rising sun on Castle Reef or Ear Mountain. In autumn, marvel at the delicate gold of the aspens and cottonwoods in the canyons of the Teton River. On a bright January day, from the high point of the Augusta/Choteau road, scan the immensity of what lies before you under a deep carpet of snow. And on a late May or June evening, west of Augusta, inhale the intoxicating aroma of millions of wildflowers that blanket the undulating hills.

Then you will know why the Rocky Mountain Front is perfect just as it is.

Prickly pear cactus.
RALPH WALDT

The Front is spectacular in any season, but spring adds the scent and beauty of wildflowers.
DOUGLASS DYE

WILDLAND AND WILDLIFE

By Gene Sentz

The history of wildlife along Montana's Front Range is closely associated with human history and the conservation movement. Diminishing game populations and their restoration has been an important factor in attitudes to save wildlands of the Front. History proves that the area's environmental and economic health depends on the well-being of its wildlife.

Native American tribes relied on game populations far back into pre-history. Wildlife sustained both their physical and spiritual lives, and Indian spirituality emphasizes the sacredness of wild places. Traditionalists still journey on vision quests and seek personal animal spirit guides just as their ancestors did. Badger Creek, Goat Mountain, Elk Pass, Antelope Butte—such place names stress the importance of wildlife along the Front.

The Blackfeet nation dominated the region when Lewis and Clark first visited. Although they had held control of the Front only since the 1700s, the Blackfeet fiercely defended it as their territory against other tribes and white intruders. Their dominance was weakened in a short time, however, both from smallpox and by the disappearance of the bison, systematically hunted almost to extinction by the whites.

Early settler Granville Stuart wrote, "It would be impossible to make persons not present on the ranges realize the rapid change that took place in three years. In 1880 the country was practically uninhabited (by people). Thousands of buffalo darkened the rolling plains. There were deer, antelope, elk, wolves, and coyotes on every hill and in every ravine and thicket...by the fall of 1883 there was not one buffalo remaining on the range and the antelope, elk, and deer were indeed scarce."

Forest ranger Ellers Koch wrote in 1941, "The South Fork of the Flathead and the Sun River country is today considered excellent game country. Deer, elk, and goats are relatively abundant. Yet in the fall of 1905 and again in 1906 I rode for a month with a pack outfit through the wildest part of that country with a rifle on my saddle, and with exception of one goat, I never saw or got a shot at a single big game animal, though grouse were fairly abundant. "

A grizzly bear foraging on rose hips.
ERWIN AND PEGGY BAUER

In 1907, the Great Falls Tribune estimated only 300 elk in the entire Sun River country. Bighorn sheep were described as "too few to count" and deer were a "remnant."

Then a great restoration began. In 1913, a diverse group of hunters, ranchers, conservationists, and public land managers convinced the Montana Legislature to establish the Sun River Game Preserve. A decade later the Montana Fish and Game Commission protected the grizzly by making it a game animal, a step toward managing a sustainable population of the great bears rather than driving them into extinction as a varmint species.

The Sun River Game Preserve and enforcement of game laws resulted in a rapid recovery of elk populations. Along the Rocky Mountain Front this became a problem of competition with domestic livestock as elk migrated out of the mountains onto foothill ranges to survive the winters. Ranchers and hunters cooperated to form the Sun River Conservation Council, which concluded that elk needed winter game range outside the mountains.

In 1947, two ranches were acquired by the Montana Fish and Game Department with special help from rancher Carl Malone, and the Sun River Game Range was established. The elk quickly learned to use it. This became the first of five state and private reserves set aside for wildlife along the Rocky Mountain Front. Others include the Ear Mountain and Blackleaf Wildlife Management Areas, The Nature Conservancy's Pine Butte Preserve, and Boone and Crockett's Theodore Roosevelt Memorial Ranch. These areas had been the buffalo pastures of the Blackfeet, then briefly were taken over as range for domestic livestock. Now they are primary wintering grounds for elk and mule deer which migrate from their mountain summer ranges to the west.

An elk population once estimated at 300 along the Front now exceeds 3,000, the second largest migratory elk herd in the nation. At least as many deer frequent the ranges, and bighorn sheep have recovered to become one of the largest herds on the continent. One of the only truly native populations of Rocky Mountain goat thrives in the high mountains from Montana's Continental Divide eastward.

12

A ranch nestles beneath Fairview Mountain.
RICK AND SUSIE GRAETZ

Good stewardship by generations of ranching

families has helped keep the *integrity*

of the Front alive.

14

The area is the last place where the grizzly regularly ventures out onto a plains environment. More than one hundred of the great bears now roam the Front, and black bears number from three to four times the grizzly population. Virtually exterminated from the area until recently, wolves have recolonized the Front on their own, moving down from Canada without being reintroduced by humans. Mountain lion numbers have steadily increased. An old-timer recently remarked, "You can't go into the Rocky Mountain Front without being watched by a lion."

The bald eagle is not uncommon, its status having improved from endangered to "threatened." Other raptors include owls, hawks, falcons, and golden eagles. The Front is a natural flyway for migrating birds, and hundreds of thousands of waterfowl move north and south in spring and autumn. "If one sees swans up near the Front, they're probably trumpeters," says a biologist. For this reason swan hunting (for tundras) is allowed only east of the highway route between Browning and Wolf Creek.

A wilderness-dependent species, the secretive harlequin duck can be observed along the high country drainages of the Front Range. Isolated native populations of westslope cutthroat trout spawn in those same remote mountain streams. And the varied species of grouse seen by Ranger Koch in the early days of the century are still "fairly abundant."

Except for the bison, every major species of flora and fauna native to Montana prior to Lewis and Clark still exists here in relatively healthy populations uncommon in other places. For this reason the Front has been called "the Serengetti of North America." The reason, of course, is its rich habitat. The Front is an ecotone, a spectacular transition between the Great Plains and the Rockies, which produces the unique and abundant mix of wildlife it harbors.

Generations of ranch families deserve much credit for a conservation ethic favorable to wintering big game herds on the large private tracts along the Front. Now, demand for recreational land encourages subdivision, which threatens to fragment habitat. Conservation easements through state agencies and private groups offer ranchers economic incentives to continue to raise livestock rather than subdivide,

A long way from its namesake, this grain elevator is testament to the strong agricultural aspect of the Front.
JIM MEPHAM

The Rocky
Mountain Front
hosts the second
largest migratory
elk herd in the
nation.
ERWIN AND PEGGY BAUER

The skies
along the Front
can often be as
spectacular as
the mountains.
RALPH WALDT

based on evidence that wildlife can coexist with cows, not condos. The hope is that continued public and private cooperation will sustain the historic trend toward protecting wildlife habitat on the Front.

Jim Posewitz, director of the Orion Hunter's Institute has written, "The lesson history teaches along the Rocky Mountain Front is that this land's greatness was realized because our predecessors accepted no boundaries. They saw land and wildlife with problems, but they put no boundaries on either their vision or their quest for solution...Their victories present us with today's opportunities...[We must] learn to think beyond boundaries and dream without bounds.

As we enter the new millennium, the continuation of the great wildlife-wildland conservation legacy of the Rocky Mountain Front/Bob Marshall country should be a primary national goal. People who know and love these magnificent landscapes firmly support that dream.

18

SOMETHING SACRED

By Gene Sentz

Aldo Leopold spoke of "a sense of place." When one comes to intimately know a special wild place, one feels the Sacred there. We touch the earth and are touched by it. We may not own the deed, but we can get very possessive of a place, especially when we become possessed by its extraordinary landscapes.

The Montana Rocky Mountain Front is my special place.

I can see fifty miles northwest from Choteau's Airport Hill across Birch Creek to Feather Woman Mountain. Seventy-five miles south of here, Caribou Peak stands above Falls Creek. Filling the spaces between are Walling Reef and Old-Man-of-the-Hills on Dupuyer Creek; Mount Frazier and Mount Werner in Blackleaf Canyon; Choteau and Baldy and Rocky and Ear mountains feeding the Teton; and Chute Mountain above Deep Creek. Castle Reef and Sawtooth guard the Sun River. Across Ford Creek, Crown Mountain and Steamboat keep watch over the Dearborn, and Scapegoat pierces the distant horizon.

The Front was "backbone of the world" to the Blackfeet and other Native Americans and to the ancients who trekked the Old North Trail. The peaks and ridges were vision quest sites. Sacred. They've been called by different names, but these same mountains and valleys remain little changed by millennia. Two centuries ago, no white man had ever seen them, yet now they are sacred in many non-Indian eyes, just as they remain to the traditionalists of the tribes.

Forest Service evaluations score the East Front of the Bob Marshall as the finest unclassified wild country in the lower 48 states, unsurpassed by any undeveloped landscape on earth. Biologists place it in the top one percent of wildlife habitat in North America. The Front is Sacred to a growing number of people.

But there are those who would like to build roads and carve mines and drill sites here to prospect for potential resources. They say it would create jobs, generate revenue, and make profits for industry stockholders.

Aspen colors below Feather Woman Mountain near the town of Heart Butte.
DOUGLASS DYE

I hold no grudge against them. Everyone in this great democracy can voice an opinion, but in this case I agree with the great majority, the 80 to 90 percent of public commenters who say, "Leave the Rocky Mountain Front alone. Save this magnificent landscape in its wild state for future generations. Let it be."

Many folks want to preserve the Front as home for eagles and elk, grizzlies and goats, jack pine and juniper, and other plants and critters, some endangered. Some economists predict long-term benefits of saving it far outweigh short-term profits gained from industrial development. Backcountry recreationists believe too many roads already intrude on public land. Some scientists urge all remaining wild country be set aside as a baseline from which to compare our mostly developed world.

There are many reasons for saving the Front, but the purest I've heard came from a Montana old-timer who told his congressman, "There are certain places on earth which should be left alone even if solid gold lies beneath them. The Rocky Mountain Front is such a place."

I agree. For me, these special mountains and valleys, in and of themselves, are reason enough. I know them. They are like brothers and sisters and cherished old friends. I keep returning to them. Always, they touch me. I suspect I am possessed by them.

Wallace Stegner described America's remaining wilderness as our "geography of hope." The wild horizons of the Rocky Mountain Front and Bob Marshall country symbolize the geography of hope for an entire continent.

It is an extraordinary land. I hope we can keep it.

Something there is Sacred.

GENE SENTZ *is a Choteau, Montana, school teacher and a fierce defender of the Front. He has gained an intimate understanding of the area through his many summers working with outfitters in the Bob Marshall Wilderness. This knowledge of the Rocky Mountain Front, and his passion for it, has gained him respect for his opinions with key decision makers.*

Sweeping view of a "small portion" of the Front from Hwy 89 between Choteau and Augusta.
RICK AND SUSIE GRAETZ

Simply put,

this is where the *plains end* and the

mountains begin.

Rodeo is not just a sport in Montana,

it is an event — a gathering of family and

friends to celebrate *a way of life*

Augusta holds
the oldest and
one of the most
popular rodeos
in Montana.
MIKE MANUEL/FAIRFIELD
SUN TIMES

TOWNS OF THE FRONT
By Rick and Susie Graetz

AUGUSTA

Five hundred people call this ranching town home. Augusta is the entryway to the Sun River Canyon area of the Front. This Rocky Mountain Front community hosts the state's oldest, and one of Montana's most popular rodeos.

It was established in the late 1860s and has always been associated with the cattle industry. Since the

late 1940s, recreation has also become an important industry in the area. Fishing, hunting, wilderness pack trips, backpacking and hiking in the nearby Bob Marshall Wilderness have brought new economic development through outfitters, guides and local dude ranches.

Both the Sun River Canyon Road, as well as the route to the Bob Marshall/ Benchmark trailhead, take off from the western edge of town.

CHOTEAU

The county seat of Teton County is one of the oldest towns in this part of Montana. In 1875 when the post office was first established, it served as a trading post called Old Agency. In 1884 the name was changed to honor Pierre Chouteau, Jr., president of the American Fur Company. He brought the first steamboat up the Missouri River. Today Choteau is an agricultural town of 1,741 people. A most attractive community, it features a wide, business-lined main street and a stately stone courthouse. Choteau prides itself as being one of the gateways to the Rocky Mountain Front and the Bob Marshall Wilderness.

It's home to the Old Trail Museum, a complex of historic area buildings and a dinosaur exhibit. The museum has a full-time curator of paleontology and conducts educational field study programs.

Seven miles north of Choteau, the Teton River Road heads toward the wall of the Rocky Mountain Front and some of the best scenery, hiking and backcountry skiing in the Front Range.

Pulitzer Prize-winning author A.B. Guthrie, Jr. lived just west of town until his death in 1991.

BYNUM

Just fourteen miles north of Choteau in Teton County, Bynum was named for the Stephen Bynum family, early settlers in the area. It's situated on the banks of Muddy Creek. In 1881 it was only a country store. The post office was established in 1885 and the first school in 1899. In 1913 the town relocated a short distance to its present site to be near the Great Northern railhead. A boom period began and the population swelled to 225 by 1916. The boom, was short-lived and the town's population began to decline as many homesteaders were forced off their land. The Great Northern Railway tracks were torn out in 1984. Roads from Bynum lead toward Muddy Creek and Blackleaf Canyon portions of The Rocky Mountain Front.

PENDROY

Pendroy is seven miles north of Bynum and two miles east of Highway 89. It was named for Levi Boots Pendroy, a Great Northern Railway employee who helped survey the area. The town was started in 1916 as a railroad branch line from Bynum. It grew quickly and was at its most prosperous level in the 1920s. Today, approximately 150 people live in the Pendroy area.

This small farming community is situated in one of the best dryland grain-growing areas in Montana and serves farmers and ranchers as a supply center.

DUPUYER

Dupuyer was originally a stage stop on the bull-team freight route between Fort Benton and Fort Browning. The town then became a supply depot for local ranchers and miners. The post office was established in 1882 and by 1903 the town had grown into a bustling commerce center. Today, this small country town has approximately 40 residents who lead a quieter lifestyle. Several roads go west from town toward the northern portions of the Rocky Mountain Front and the trailheads into the Bob Marshall and Great Bear Wilderness areas. One of them ends at Swift Dam and the Birch Creek trailheads.

HEART BUTTE

This Pondera county community is located on the Blackfeet Indian Reservation and is the closest town on the Front to the wall of mountains. It was named for nearby mountains that look like inverted hearts. The post office was established in 1915. Approximately 500 people call Heart Butte home.

Small, pleasant,

unobtrusive communities are set well

to the east of the mountains.

Wheat farms
surround the town
of Bynum.
CHUCK HANEY

All who live and play

here have a serious responsibility to respect

and protect this special land.

Steamboat Mountain
rides the crests of
the Rocky Mountain
Front southwest
of Augusta.
RICK AND SUSIE GRAETZ

It's located well off of Highway 89 and can be reached from Dupuyer and several points north of there.

BROWNING

Named for a US Commissioner of Indian Affairs, Browning is the agency headquarters for the Blackfeet Indian Reservation. Located at the junction of Hwy 2 and Hwy 89, and only 18 miles from Glacier National Park, it is a tourist stop for gas and snacks and home to about 4,500 full-time residents.

The Blackfeet National Bank, established in 1987, was the first and only tribally controlled, reservation-based, full-service, commercial bank in the United States. Fully accredited since 1985, the Blackfeet Community College provides a means for a better way of life. This busy, mostly Native American town is home to the excellent Museum of the Plains Indians. The Tribal Council is working in conjunction with the Nature Conservancy of Montana to protect reservation lands. There has been a post office here since 1900.

EAST GLACIER

Located on Hwy 2 and serving the southeast entrance to the Park, East Glacier is the only town along the Front that sits hard-up against the mountains.

This colorful burg has approximately 600 full-time residents. Most are professionals who work in the Browning schools and hospital or for the National Park Service. During the tourist season the population swells to about 2,500 folks.

Extensive gardens lead from the chalet-style Amtrak train depot to the grand and historic Glacier Park Lodge with its wonderful lobby pillared by enormous four-story-tall Douglas fir logs.

BABB AND ST. MARY

On Hwy 89, heading to the Canadian border, the small hamlets of Babb and St. Mary both access Glacier National Park. Life here mainly revolves around provisions for Park visitors. St. Mary is a main entrance on the Going-to-the-Sun Hwy. Babb, further north, is a pass-through for those on their way to Many Glacier or Waterton Lakes National Park.

Sawtooth Ridge
in the Sun River
area.
RICK AND SUSIE GRAETZ

Seasons change,

but the *breathtaking beauty*

of these mountains remains constant.

Badger Creek on
the 1.5 million-acre
Blackfeet Reservation.
JOHN LAMBING

Aspen groves add
texture and color
to the mountains
and hillsides of the
Front.
GEORGE WUERTHNER

The classic
St. Mary Lake in
Glacier National
Park on the
northern most
reaches of the
Rocky Mountian
Front.
RICK AND SUSIE GRAETZ

 Three layers
in the mist...
Ear Mountain,
an unnamed ridge,
Rocky Mountain
Peak.
LARRY MAYER

A waterfowl landing
strip between East
Glacier and
Browning.
RICK AND SUSIE GRAETZ

Rampart-like
reefs guard the
Bob Marshall
Wilderness.
JOHN LAMBING

The aspens may think it's spring, but winter still holds sway in the high country of the South Fork of the Teton River.
RICK AND SUSIE GRAETZ

Rockwell Falls in the Two Medicine Valley of Glacier National Park.
CHUCK HANEY

There is no need to choose,

this place has it all…prairie,

wildlife, mountains and a spiritual sense.

Bighorn Sheep
head towards the
base of Castle
Reef near Gibson
Reservoir.
JIM MEPHAM

The Sun River at
Hannan Gulch as
it leaves the Rocky
Mountain Front.
RICK AND SUSIE GRAETZ

Browning.
RICK AND SUSIE GRAETZ

Freezeout Lake,
outside of Choteau
on the prairie, is an
important stopover
for millions of
migrating birds.
RANDY BEACHAM

The tipi village
on Egg Mountain.
Located on the
Pine Butte Preserve,
the area harbors
one of the richest
paleontological
finds of the century,
Maiasaura
Peeblesorum.
RICK AND SUSIE GRAETZ

The Badger-Two
Medicine area from
Tubby Creak.
GEORGE WUERTHNER

45

46

A prairie pond
and Haystack
Butte from the
Benchmark Road.
RICK AND SUSIE GRAETZ

49

Willow Creek area.
JOHN REDDY

Arrowleaf
balsamroot on
the southern end
of the Front.
JOHN REDDY

A truly amazing landscape...

at once peaceful and exciting, subtle and grand,

wild and settled, preserved yet endangered.

A favorite fishing
spot is Bean Lake.
RICK AND SUSIE GRAETZ

Sawtooth Ridge
and the entrance
to Sun River
Canyon.
RICK AND SUSIE GRAETZ

Hikers enjoying the
view above
Hannan Gulch.
RICK AND SUSIE GRAETZ

The Sun River
Game Range is
one of five state
and two private
wildlife preserves
on the Front.
RICK AND SUSIE GRAETZ

54

Alongside
the Blackfeet
Reservation,
Feather Woman
Mountain left,
and Mowitch
Basin center.
RICK AND SUSIE GRAETZ

Quiet lakes nestle
like jewels among
the mountaintops.
RALPH WALDT

Marmot Peak
on the South Fork
of the Teton.
RALPH WALDT

Shimmering waters

and *towering cliffs* capture the eye

and imagination in one.

The Cut Bank
Valley beneath
Mad Wolf and
Bad Marriage
mountains, Glacier
National Park.
CHUCK HANEY

Elk, bighorn sheep,
antelope and other
animals such as
these fawn mule
deer twins now
flourish on the
Front.
ERWIN AND PEGGY BAUER

Cascading waterfall
on the way to
Headquarters Pass.
RICK AND SUSIE GRAETZ

Chances are, you can walk into

any business in these small towns and

shake the hand of the owner.

Choteau is the
Teton County seat.
RICK AND SUSIE GRAETZ

Cooling off by the
crystal waters of
the scenic
Dearborn River.
RICK AND SUSIE GRAETZ

View from
south of Augusta
sweeping north.
RICK AND SUSIE GRAETZ

Fly-fishing, prairie
pothole style.
RICK AND SUSIE GRAETZ

Bountiful gardens
and the East
Glacier Lodge.
RICK AND SUSIE GRAETZ

A wildflower
serenade near
East Glacier.
DOUGLASS DYE

The Sun River
Game Range is
important big
game wintering
habitat.
RICK AND SUSIE GRAETZ

Dudes and hunters
alike use horsepack
trips to get into the
backcountry. Below
Rocky Mountain
Peak on the
Headquarters Pass
Trail.
GEORGE WUERTHNER

Whether by foot, horse or car,

get out and visit its

open and hidden places.

The Pine Butte
Guest Ranch owned
by the Nature
Conservancy of
Montana is one
of several dude
ranches along the
Front.
RICK AND SUSIE GRAETZ

St. Mary Bridge
and the mountains
around St. Mary
Lake just inside
Glacier National
Park.
RICK AND SUSIE GRAETZ

The state-owned Ear
Mountain Wildlife
Management Area.
RICK AND SUSIE GRAETZ

76

The Swift
Reservoir out
of Dupuyer.
RICK AND SUSIE GRAETZ

At 9,392 feet,
Rocky Mountain
Peak is the highest
summit on the
Front and in the
Bob Marshall
Wilderness.
RICK AND SUSIE GRAETZ

Peaks and ridges once were, and still are,

used as Indian vision quest sites.

Pine Butte out
of Choteau.
RICK AND SUSIE GRAETZ

The Front has *many friends...*

it is not only Native Americans who

consider it sacred.

Young Blackfeet
dancers wait
to perform.
RICK AND SUSIE GRAETZ

Ground blizzards
often make
backroad travel
an adventure.
RICK AND SUSIE GRAETZ

Bison once again
roam the prairies
of the Rocky
Mountain Front.
RICK AND SUSIE GRAETZ

Mt. Werner and
Mt. Frazier in the
Birch Creek area.
RICK AND SUSIE GRAETZ

Ranching is
the major
economic activity
on the Front.
JOHN LAMBING

The Front has often been referred

to as "America's Serengetti."

Serenity comes at
dawn on the Two
Medicine Bison
Ranch near Kiowa
and Glacier
National Park.
RICK AND SUSIE GRAETZ

Choteau Mountain.
RICK AND SUSIE GRAETZ

From the Sun
River Canyon Road
looking south to
Haystack Butte.
RICK AND SUSIE GRAETZ

Escape to Arizona
foiled by fence.
RICK AND SUSIE GRAETZ

East face of
Castle Reef.
RICK AND SUSIE GRAETZ

ROCKY MOUNTAIN FRONT

Legend

- ☐ National Forests
- ☐ National Park
- ☐ Wilderness
- ☐ Unprotected Roadless Lands
- ☐ Wildlife Preserves

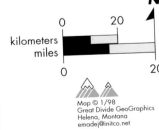

kilometers
miles

0   20

0   20

N

Map © 1/98
Great Divide GeoGraphics
Helena, Montana
emadej@initco.net

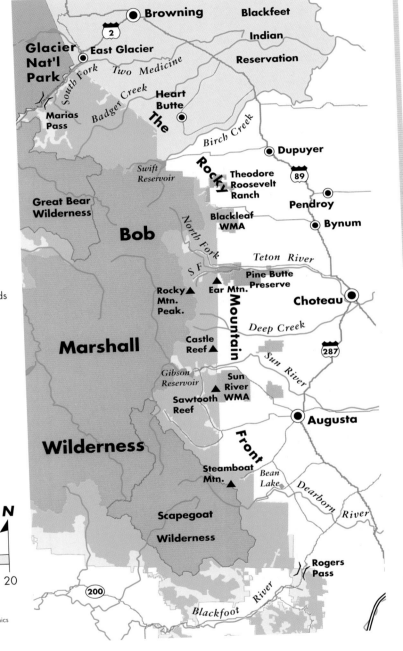

Browning

Blackfeet

Glacier Nat'l Park   East Glacier

Indian

South Fork   *Two Medicine*

Reservation

Marias Pass   *Badger Creek*

Birch Creek

Heart Butte

The

Dupuyer

Swift Reservoir

Great Bear Wilderness

Rocky

Theodore Roosevelt Ranch

Bob

North Fork

Blackleaf WMA

Pendroy

Bynum

Teton River

S F

Pine Butte Preserve

Rocky Mtn. Peak. ▲   **Ear Mtn.** ▲

Mountain

Choteau

Marshall

Castle Reef ▲

Deep Creek

Gibson Reservoir

Sun River WMA ▲

Sun River

Sawtooth Reef

Front

Augusta

Wilderness

Steamboat Mtn. ▲

Bean Lake

Dearborn River

Scapegoat

Wilderness

Rogers Pass

Blackfoot River

Blackfoot